NEUROTICA

IMAGES OF THE BIZARRE

NEUROTICA

IMAGES OF THE BIZARRE BY
J·K·POTTER

INTRODUCTION BY

Lydia Lunch

Paper Tiger

An imprint of Dragon's World

Dragon's World Ltd

Limpsfield, Surrey RH8 0DY, Great Britain

First published by Dragon's World Ltd 1996

Editor Helen Williams

Designer Ken Wilson

Editorial Director Pippa Rubinstein

Art Director John Strange

ISBN 1 85028 359 1

Printed in Singapore

Frontispiece

𝒢irl from Interzone

Private work. The insect component of this picture is a cicada or locust shell, the slightly translucent exoskeleton
which is left behind after metamorphosis. The title is from William Burroughs.

[1994]

CONTENTS

Lydia Lunch
INTRODUCTION

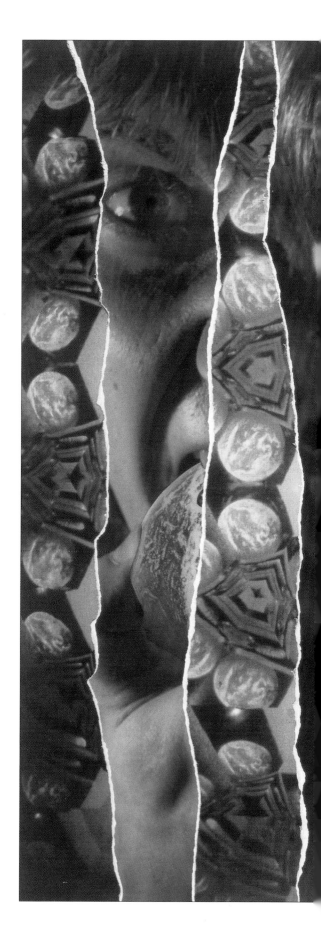

*R*EAL HORROR

rises up to greet me with the passing of each new day. I wake to find the same outdated soul-searing power structures still pillaging, plundering and raping the entire planet. World-wide war rages. We all suffer the consequences. More than 60 per cent of the Earth's population live in abject poverty, mostly women and children. Female infanticide is the favoured form of birth control in the most severely populated countries. Slave labour proliferates. Minimum wage isn't paying anyone's rent. Social services are being slashed on a global level. Defence budgets boom. Education plummets. Violence escalates. Incarceration skyrockets. Pollution and global warming turn the entire planet into a toxic waste dump. Yet, instead of dealing with the Real Issues, 'the Pornography of Reality', we are still enslaved to tyrannical overlords who are more concerned with the 'dangerous messages' supposedly sent forth from music, movies, television and literature, who continue to attempt to limit the scope of our creative freedoms, fearing the fantastical expressions of artistic angst as if it were a moral plague sent to taint the masses. The brutality of real events, condensed and twisted as they are (before we receive even the twenty-second soundbites on the evening news), are far more horrifying than even the most demented visionaries' outlandish rumblings. To accuse art, literature or music of being the antagonist in the fall of our culture is to once again blame the victim, a technique of blatant scapegoating which pre-dates even the Crucifixion, and forces us to once more ask the question: Is art imitating life, does life imitate art, or are we suffering from a confused intermingling of the two?

The role of the artist is to give voice and vision to the frustrations and fantasies which haunt their day to day. I use words and rants like power tools, deconstructing 'phallacies', inaccuracies and the lie of the American dream, in order to vent vitriol

Good God Let's Eat

This picture of a man taking a bite out of the Earth was inspired by
the short story 'Cain Rose Up' by Stephen King.

[1995]

7

Introduction

at a Big Brother Bureaucracy whose only concern for the individual is how much control they have over him. J. K. Potter commands his visions to scour the fleshy underbelly of a fantastical netherworld, desperately seeking to escape a world made all too (un)Real by enemy forces who cloak genocidal tendencies with false morality; creating dreamscapes where wildly liberated women are encouraged to fully embrace their feral nature, transcending the confines of the here and now, the prison of the human form, and soaring beyond into another dimension where limitations are banished, because in Fantasy all is permitted. There are no restrictions. We all need a place to escape to, in this the day of ever tightening strangleholds, where we are all strapped for cash, confined in cubicles, herded like sheep, counted like cattle, contagious and under surveillance.

Entering into the world of *Neurotica*, we are forced to leave expectations behind. Leg and limb intertwine in a glorious jumble of disjointed union, forcing us to question the genetic code which mass-produces the human body with such little divergence. J. K. Potter strives to improve upon Nature, who turned lazy with human creation, after designing a spectacular multiplicity of plumed birds, furry beasts, tentacled creatures, and flora and fauna of breathtaking glory, but left our species devoid of the exotic, favouring brain and brawn over beauty which is unique. Potter relocates our mythical forebears unlocking the sacred mysteries which married superhuman and animal nature to the gods and goddesses, whose mystical powers transcended those of mere mortals. Transposing our true fears of our elemental nature upon his twisted visions of a return to a mutated Eden, Potter lures us into a *Neurotica* whose inhabitants embrace a terrifying beauty and horrifying grace, and delight in their escape to a timeless wonderland, where the shackles which limit the body and soul are forever lifted, freeing them at last to experience a unique splendour usually reserved for daydreams and nightmares.

To collaborate with J. K. Potter exhilarates the senses which are too often pummelled to near oblivion by the onslaught of rules, regulations and an outdated code of ethics. Through his creations he unhinges his psyche and libido, giving them free rein to traverse the perverse landscapes which people his overactive imaginings, allowing us through his visions to wander a terrain where flesh, fur and feather commingle. Divorce your inhibitions, shed preconceptions and allow yourself to wander: *Neurotica* awaits you...

LYDIA LUNCH, 1995

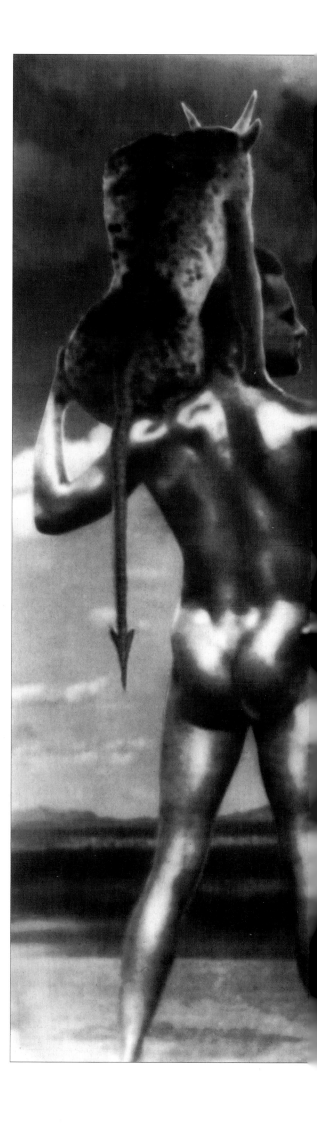

Lydia and Ubermenschen
Private Work.
[1995]

JK

I'll never forget the state fairs and carnival sideshows I witnessed as a boy growing up in Alabama. The freak shows were my favourite, but somehow the living freaks never quite impressed me as much as the dead ones. It was the two-headed farm animals, three-eyed cats and other deformed abominations, floating in rows of large glass jars filled with liquid, that fascinated me. At one particularly memorable sideshow exhibit, I saw an unusual series of creations that could only have been made by an artist who had dexterously sewn together the flesh of different species. How else could you have a fetal pig with the head of an albino catfish? As I pressed my nose close to the jar, I saw rows of fine stitching and my mind reeled at the thought of some mad artisan sewing the parts of dead animals together, peeling the flesh off one wet cadaver and stretching it partially over another. I could easily envision some crazy old man hunched over his macabre work in a woodshed full of jars — his eyes distorted by the large magnifying glass one would obviously need to do such detailed work. Perhaps I had seen too many Hammer horror films at the time, but this image has never left me; neither has the image of a dead puppy with the head of a mole, floating upside-down in a jar.

Since then I have encountered some creative taxidermists who have done similar work, but nothing quite equals those early memories of that sideshow Victor Frankenstein.

To me the grotesque is beautiful, the weird sublime, and the macabre a rare and delectable vintage wine. Gargoyles clinging to the buttresses of Gothic cathedrals are as cute as kittens to me, especially the ones devouring human beings. Cemeteries are always delightfully pleasant places in which to loiter — some are veritable outdoor art galleries. Morbid Mexican Day of the Dead art, New England tombstone carvings of stylized winged skulls, and demonic-looking African masks are always lovely to behold, though some folks might not think so. The writer Georges Bataille thought that the aftermath of a fatal car crash could be beautiful, though I wouldn't carry it that far. I'm not the kind of person who thrills to the sight of autopsy pictures or grisly crime scene photos, though dissections of bog people or Egyptian mummies are always of interest. I would hate to miss one of those.

Halloween is my favourite holiday, but I rarely celebrate it on 31 October — I suppose I celebrate it all year long. However, there are those narrow-minded souls among us who consider even the observance of Halloween to be the vilest heresy. While these people, who see the Devil in every corner can vegetate at the edges of existence, I remain engrossed with every three-eyed Balinese monster mask and Kwakiutl totem pole I encounter. It is in this spirit that I continue my own work, though I would never claim that my images are as important as the objets d'art I have mentioned above. The pictures in this book are only the gratuitous fantasies of one man obsessed with the bizarre, the unusual and grotesque.

Chapter One

« GROTESQUERIE »

Heels
Over Head
Private work. I frequently
have nightmares where human bodies
are reconfigured in disturbing ways.
This is an image from
one of them.
[1992]

*B*rain Laid Bare
Private work. Portrait of actor and long-time
collaborator Alan Bernhoft, who has an extensive
repertoire of startling facial contortions
which I have found very inspiring
over the years.
[1990]

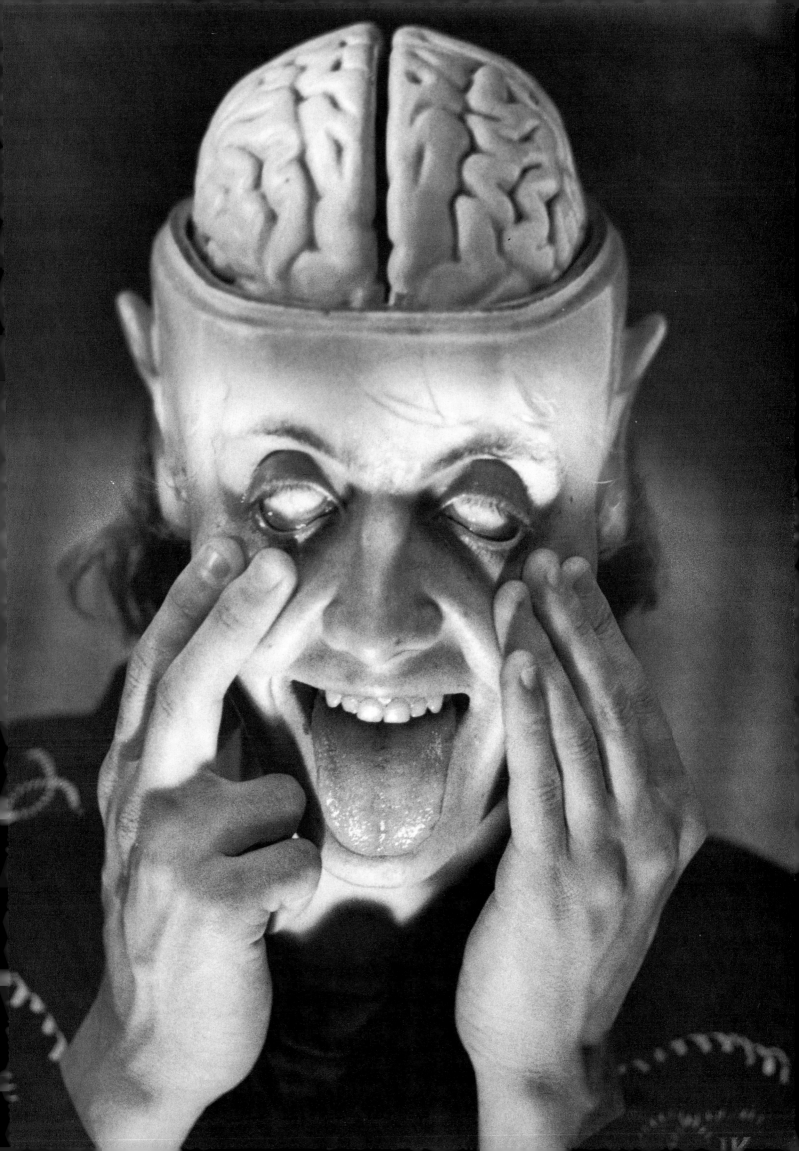

Hunger for Horror

Paperback book cover for
an anthology of horror stories
about food. Daw Books.
[1988]

Something Nasty

Illustration for a short story of the same
title by William F. Nolan, from the anthology
Things Beyond Midnight, Scream/Press.
I am always reminded of this picture
whenever I have a sore throat.
[1984]

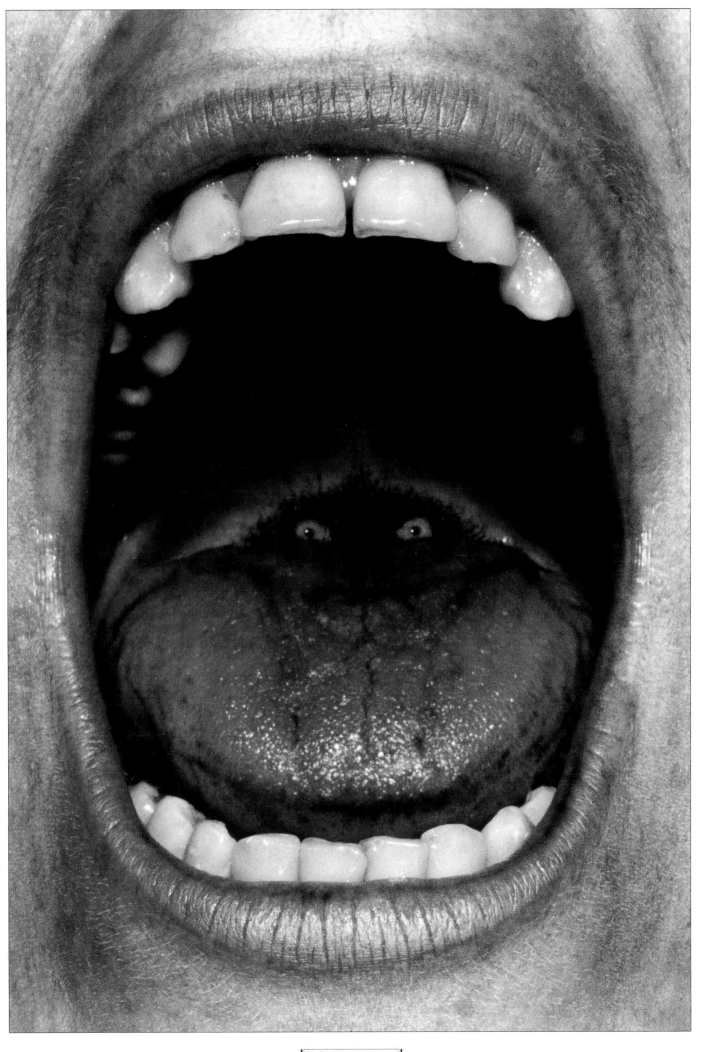

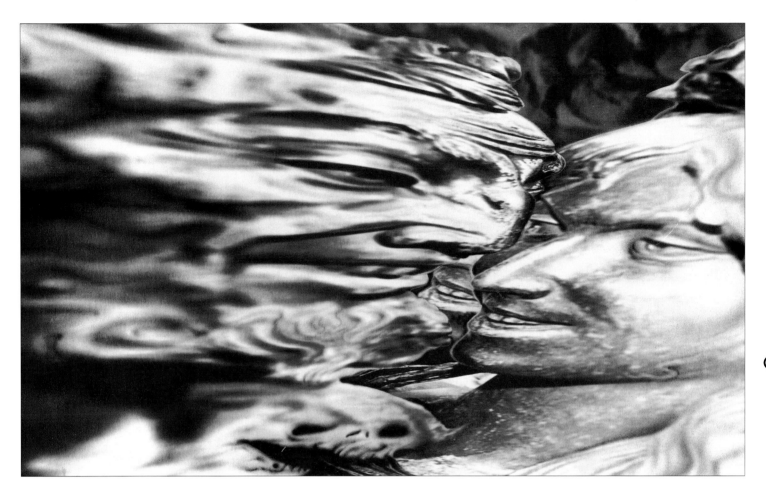

Dolls

Illustration for 'Dolls',
a story of sex and satanism
by the master horror writer
Ramsey Campbell.
From the book
Scared Stiff,
Warner Books.
[1987]

The
Devil's
Mistress

An alternative
endpaper design
for Scared Stiff.
[1987]

Fashion '95: Supermodel in a Pigsty

Private work. Symbolic of the fashion world as I view it. I suppose mud-splattered skin was probably one of the first fashion statements of primitive man.

[1995]

Three-Faced

Private work. I knew he was two-faced, but when I realized that his girlfriend exerted such a strong influence on his personality that she was able to speak through him, I concluded that he was in fact three-faced.

[1994]

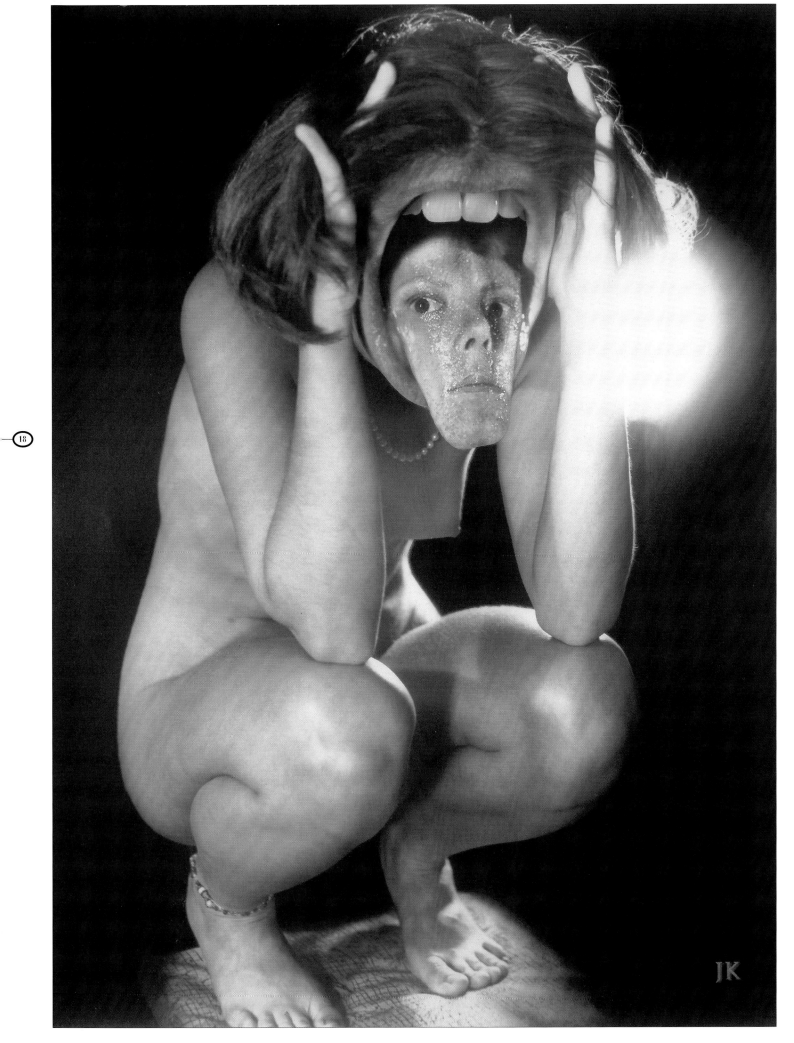

Tongue Visage

Private work. She regurgitated
her own face in a paroxysm
of oral-instigated neurosis.
It was not a pretty sight.
[1991]

ℱans and Pros

Private work. The dark side of fandom
rears its ugly head(s) in this nightmare image
brought on by attending too many
science fiction conventions
in a short time span.
[1992]

*V*R
Syndrome
Private work.
Virtual reality abuse
can lead to
the manifestation of
some very unpleasant
symptoms.
[1992]

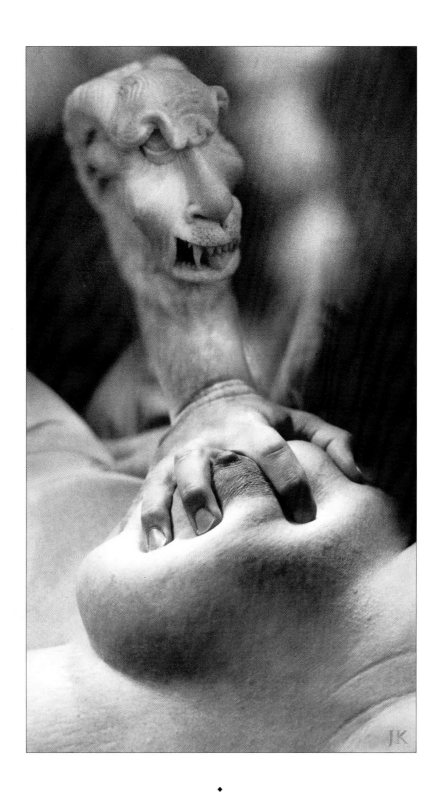

𝓜r. Morbus
Private work. Rob is very
proud of his rare skin condition,
which hasn't been seen
since the Middle Ages.
[1995]

Gropius
Private work. Gropius is
an odd little fellow
with some strange habits
that are probably best
left unviewed by
ordinary mortals.
[1993]

Yee Haw!
Private work, inspired by
the disturbing rural denizens
of H.P. Lovecraft's story
'Shadows Over
Innsmouth'.
[1994]

*T*he
Inquisitor
Private work.
The metal mask
in this picture
is an actual medieval
torture mask
that I photographed
in the Tower
of London.
[1995]

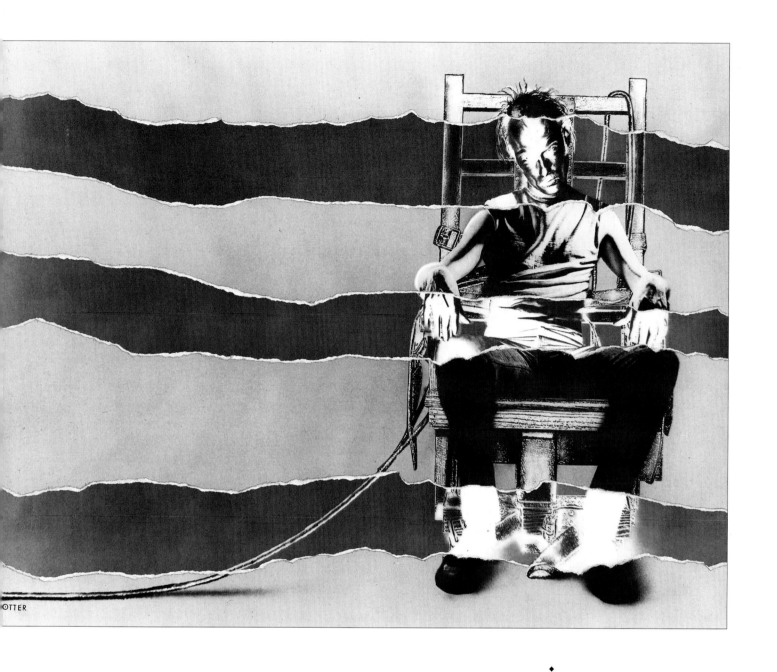

OTTER

The Chair

Endpaper design
and illustration for
the horror story 'The Chair'
by Dennis Etchison,
from the book Red Dreams.
The model in this picture
is Hector Plasmic,
a friend I always suspected
would eventually wind up
in a real electric chair.
Scream/Press
[1984]

The Face That Must Die

This picture illustrates the line
'He stared at the razor
as though it might direct him',
from Ramsey Campbell's
slasher novel of the same title.
The graffiti was fortuitously
provided by vandals who
did quite a decorative job
on the ruined house
where this picture
was taken.
Scream/Press.
[1983]

Obeahman

Private work. I found the African mask partially depicted in this picture in a used book store, where it had been squirrelled away in a box filled with Nazi regalia, evidently souvenirs collected by some veteran of the African campaigns in World War II.

[1994]

The Pure Product

The pure products of America go on a crazy crime spree in this illustration for the John Kessel short story of the same title, from the book Meeting in Infinity, Arkham House.

[1992]

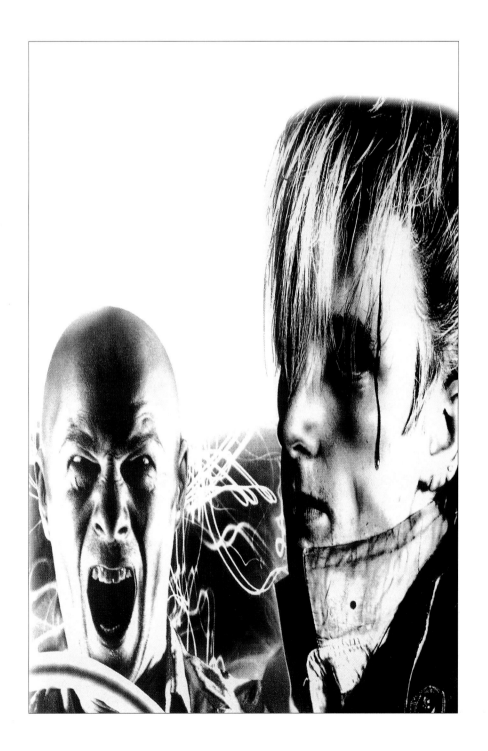

Stumpface

Private work. The fantastic
whorled patterns on the surface
of this dead tree suggested a face
even before I superimposed
the image of the girl.

[1995]

Severed Tryst

Private work. Lydia Lunch cradles
the head of her beautiful friend Carla
during a photosession in an old
New Orleans cemetery.

[1993]

Why Not
You and I?

This torn image, which strips away
the flesh to reveal the bones underneath,
was designed to grace the cover of
a collection of horror stories by
the late Karl Edward Wagner.
Tor Books.
[1988]

Hand of the
Grannygnasher

This concept was created for
film producer/director Brian Yuzna
for use in a film. This was supposed
to be constructed in latex over
an articulated framework and used
in a scene where it would bite
someone's head off.
[1993]

JK

Greetings from Shoggoth Rock

Private work. A novelty postcard from a very exotic location that's guaranteed to impress the folks back home when they see it.
[1995]

Attack of the Yithian

Private work. The monster in this picture is food sculpture made with rotting eggplant and canned octopus tentacles, with a glass eye for garnish.
[1995]

Bored in the USA

Private work. They say that rock and roll will never die, but sometimes I wish it would; especially when I hear the same guitar solos I heard as a teenager recycled over and over again by less than original musicians. This piece expresses my personal feelings with precision.

[1995]

American Zombie

This was created for a book of gratuitously sick zombie stories by Douglas E. Winter, a marvellously demented writer, who works for a law firm that specializes in litigation on the behalf of plane crash victims. Borderlands Press.

[1995]

JK

Warped Lucinda

Private work. Lucinda is going soft and her self-perceptions are sliding further and further into an elastic world of dementia that threatens to melt her self-image and estrange her from reality once and for all.

[1994]

Flibbertigibbet's Revenge

Private work. He was paralyzed with fear as the flibbertigibbet scampered across his chest to perch on his face, where she could be warmed by his breath.

[1995]

Terrors of
the New Flesh
Private work.
This woman is depicted
at the precise moment
that she realizes
the nightmare is
in control.
[1994]

The
Warped Ones
Private work. A liquescent
and distorted portrait
created by double exposing
two different images
reflected in a warped
mirrored surface.
[1992]

I believe in ghosts. Ghosts stalk the rubble of ancient ruined castles and walk the halls of towering modern office buildings. The ghost of Joseph Stalin shuffles through the Kremlin. Ghosts of extinct Carolina parakeets swarm in the night sky, their sweet faces haunting us with the memory of their slaughter. Ghosts of dead actors haunt your television, re-enacting the same old scenes over and over again in a flickering black and white purgatory. If you don't believe in ghosts I can only pity you because, metaphorically speaking, our lives are crowded with swirling wraiths, ghosts and spectres crying out for our attention.

I readily admit that I have never photographed a ghost that I didn't create myself through the machinations of special effects photography. I have long been amused by Victorian spirit photographs, some of which are so contrived as to be laughable. Some of those crude double exposures of people covered with sheets, questionable seances, and mediums frothing ectoplasm that looks remarkably like pastry dough, are classics of early photo manipulation.

Not all of these spirit photographs are laughable though; the occasional more convincing example is always soul-stirring, regardless of whether it is fake or not. I consider those early Victorian spirit photographs as an influence on my own.

Decrepit old houses and lonely ruined factories, partially reclaimed by nature, are some of my favourite

places to take pictures. Exploring old unsafe buildings can be a very dangerous business though; you never know when the floor might collapse beneath you, or who or what you might encounter in these crumbling desolate places.

I remember one abandoned, partially burned down amusement park that I visited late at night as a summer storm approached. Twisted, fire-damaged metal girders were groaning in a strong wind and a large section of the skeletal structure came crashing down in the darkness with an impressive shower of sparks. It was a chilling sight, especially since I had walked beneath that area just scant minutes before.

Once while I was exploring an old ruined building I opened a closet door, to surprise a bum who was apparently leaning against the door as he slept, because he tumbled right out at my feet. I don't know which of us was more disturbed by this encounter, as we both yelled simultaneously. It seemed like an hour before my heart stopped racing.

Another time, while trespassing on private land in an effort to photograph an old, overgrown family cemetery, a farmer turned his dogs loose on me and I was chased up a tree by slavering pit bulls.

I've been beaten up, threatened, shot at, detained by police, scratched by barb wire and stung all over by bees, in my efforts to take photos that I just couldn't resist. Fortunately my foolhardy days of illegal trespass and even worse forms of risky behaviour have now given way to a somewhat more restrained approach to both photography and life.

Chapter Two
«HAUNTED·PLACES»

*E*vil in the Attic

This image, originally the cover design for The Influence by Ramsey Campbell, remained unpublished until it was bought by a publisher who used it on the cover of Evil in the Attic, Avon Books.
|1995|

*T*he Companion

Illustration for the classic short story 'The Companion' by Ramsey Campbell. Campbell himself took me to a Liverpool amusement arcade where he pointed out this ghost train as being similar to the one in his story. The figures were added later. From the book Alone With the Horrors, Arkham House.
|1993|

The Lamia

Private work. The lamia
Morthylla, from Clark Ashton
Smith's story 'Morthylla',
is standing before an ornate
Gothic pulpit from the
Victoria and Albert Museum,
London.
[1993]

Morthylla

Private work. Previously unpublished illustration again inspired
by Clark Ashton Smith's story.
The beautiful elaborate tomb in
the background
was photographed in
the wonderful Père Lachaise
cemetery in Paris.
[1993]

Voice of
the Beach

A hallucinatory illustration
for a Ramsey Campbell story
of the same title from
Alone With the Horrors,
Arkham House.
[1993]

*T*he
Feeding Place

Private work. This is the interior
of a wonderfully constructed old barn
which I found in a lonely and
uninhabited woodland area
in North Louisiana.
[1986]

**Ghost and
Sepulchres**
Private work. A ghostly
figure stands before
a crumbling society tomb
in an old cemetery.
[1991]

**Queen of
Lincoln Beach**
Private work. The ruins of Lincoln Beach
are a legacy of the time when segregated
beaches and amusement parks thrived
along the shores of Lake Ponchatrain
in New Orleans, Louisiana.
[1995]

The Sybil
Private work. A portrait of
Lydia Lunch reflected in
the mirror of her dressing table,
which also appears on
the opposite page.
[1993]

Vanity
Private work. A young woman
is so entranced by her own mirrored
image that she becomes as one
with her reflection.
[1993]

**ℱace to Face
with Herself**
Private work.
Lydia Lunch caught in the
narcissistic throes of ghostly
self-embrace. An unretouched
double exposure.
[1993]

Coffin Rick
Private work. Portrait of
undertaker and coffin collector
Rick Staton, who also deals
in the art of serial killers
and other miscreants.
[1993]

aunting Women

Cover for an anthology of ghost stories
written by great female practitioners of
the trade. This loosely illustrates
'The Yellow Wallpaper'
by Charlotte Perkins Gilman.

[1989]

Triumvirate

Private work. When I overlapped the negatives
of these two skulls, another more sinister
image formed between them. I then brought out
this central image in the final print with a little
airbrush touch-up and colour.

[1985]

Fantazius Mallare

Private work. This piece and its companion
on the opposite page were inspired by
Ben Hecht's first book, Fantazius Mallare,
a long-time favourite of mine.

[1988]

*V*ictims
of Memory

Private work. The blurred figure
of Hecht's character Mallare
appears in the background
of these images.

[1993]

Wraith
at Plas Teg

Private work.
This ghostly photo
was taken at Plas Teg,
which has the reputation
of being the most
haunted house
in Wales.
[1993]

Horror House

Private work. This old Victorian
mansion with its raw, unpainted
cypress wood exterior always
had a menacing look to it,
so I thought I would intensify this
by superimposing a skull onto
its circular porches.
[1994]

Barataria Landscape

Private work. Barataria is located in Louisiana bayou country south of
New Orleans. This picture depicts a beautiful crumbling cherub from an old
country cemetery and a lonely mossman whose mournful cries
mingle with the sound of the wind.

[1982]

Honey Island Swamp Fever-Dream

Private work. I found this incredible tree deep in Mississippi's Honey Island
Swamp, a haunted place that has spawned many monstrous legends.
The tree inspired the finished image.

[1995]

The ancient Egyptians represented the god Anubis as a jackal-headed man, the god Thoth as part man, part ibis, and the goddess Hathor as having the head of a cow. The Hindu deity Garuda is often depicted as a man with the head and legs of an eagle, and Ganesha is part human, part elephant. Some of the earliest cave paintings depict men with antlers, the heads of horses, and the paws of bears. Hybrid human and animal forms abound in the religion and art of all eras. There is a seemingly endless variety of examples, from centaur and sphinx to minotaur and mermaid. Why are animal attributes given to the gods? Do these strange amalgamations of different species symbolize the world of instinct as it relates to the power of human will, as some psychologists have theorized, or do they represent the complex and inter-related nature of all creatures on this planet?

The answers to these questions are varied and complicated. I have long been fascinated by the mythical creatures of antiquity, and this has inspired me to create my own personal mythological pantheon that includes piranha men, insect women, armadillo gods and other decidedly less wholesome creations. Sometimes people remind me of animals in their behaviour and appearance, and animals can exhibit very human qualities as well. A young giraffe's graceful movements reminded me of a dancer of equal grace who I had photographed, so I combined their forms. The monkey man in *Small Town Menagerie* (see page 69) was created after I noticed negatives in my files of a man and a monkey that corresponded exactly in size and facial proportion. I simply sandwiched the two negatives together and printed them as one. The final effect was unnerving. I once met a young lady who exhibited behaviour that inexplicably reminded me of an insect. Why I thought that is probably a matter ripe for psychiatric inquiry. These impressions inspired the image titled *Girl From Interzone* (see frontispiece), though the model I used was not the original source of inspiration. The egret-armed *Aviana* (see page opposite) seemed appropriate since the ancient Egyptians emulated the movements of birds with their arms while dancing. Other images, such as the part man, part chihuahua (see page 68), are novelty postcard pieces done strictly as jokes. That fellow in no way reminded me of a chihuahua!

Chapter Three

«ZOOMORPHIC MENAGERIE»

Bird of
**Another Feather
(Detail)**
Private work.
This is but one in a series of
pictures of avian coiffures
that I have created.
[1992]

Aviana
Private work. When model Katrina Uribe
spontaneously struck this pose, the idea for
the finished piece immediately sprang
into my head.
[1994]

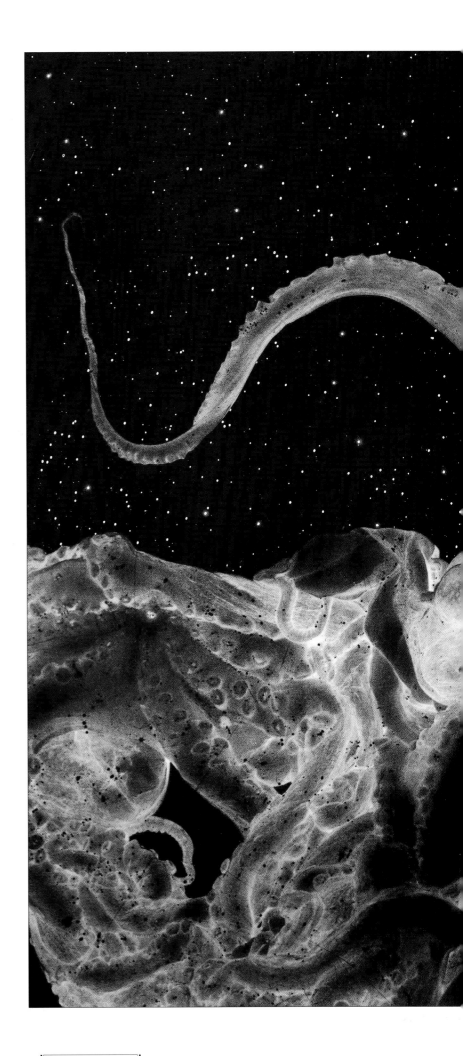

Xeethra

Private work. After
I photographed the octopus
used to create this image,
I cooked and ate it with
a nice red sauce.

[1993]

Mouth of
the Maw Shark

Private work. Another disturbing image
dredged from the depths of a nightmare.
I did a quick sketch of this concept
immediately upon waking.

[1995]

*T*hree
Friends

Private work.
The faces of three
of my closest cronies
are warped and
mutilated in
this affectionate
group portrait.

[1994]

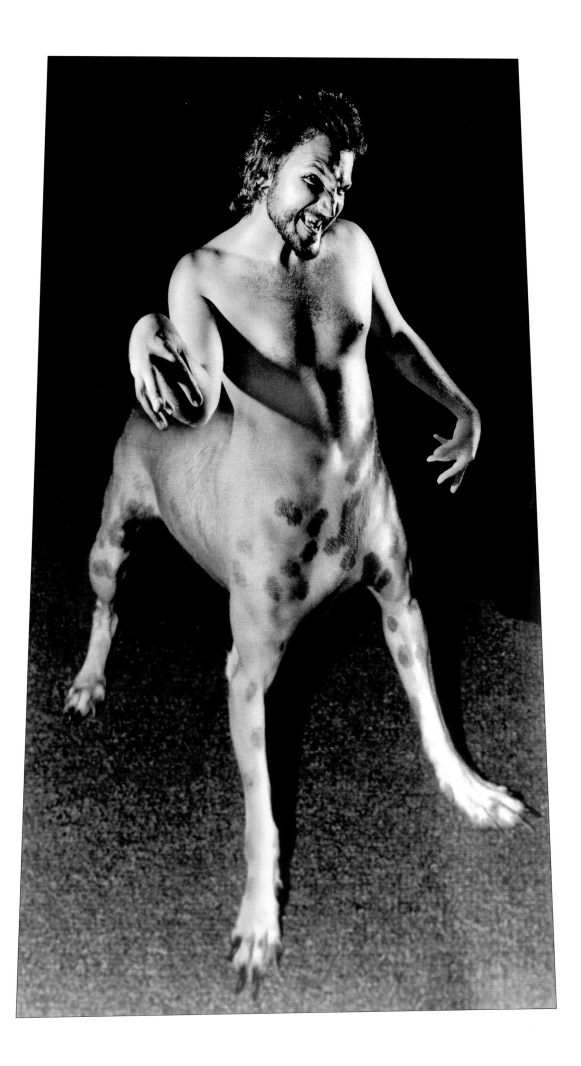

Chihuahua Man

Private work. Originally I intended to transform this man into a satyr, but I decided to try something a little more outré.

[1993]

Small Town Menagerie

Private work. These gentlemen had certain characteristics that reminded me of the creatures they now represent.

[1994]

Mr Armand Dillo

Private work. Irreverent portrait of Reverend Ivan Stang, one of the founders of the Church of the Sub-Genius, which promotes the use of 'short-duration personal saviours' of your own choosing.

[1992]

Armadillo God

Private work. I've been fascinated with armadillos ever since my first encounter with one as a boy. I accidentally collided with one while riding my bicycle at night. I was scraped and bruised from falling, but the armadillo, who had curled into a tight ball, rolled away and escaped unharmed.

[1984]

Bird of
Another
Feather

Private work. The border design
for this image contains the
repetitive form of a small animal
skull photographed through a
homemade kaleidoscope.
[1992]

*P*irahnaman

Private work. Another
concept loosely inspired by
H.P.Lovecraft's 'Shadows
Over Innsmouth'.
[1985]

***Z*ebra Centauress Watching Ostrich Sex**

Private work. This startling scene of ostrich sex was photographed early one morning at a zoo. The female ostrich was absolutely passive while the male spread his wings, swung his head back and forth like a metronome, and made the most God-awful noises I have ever heard. The zebra woman was added to the picture later.

[1993]

*A*ngel

Private work. Inspired by the extraordinary model Katrina Uribe, one of my favourite collaborators. Katrina, who appears numerous times in this book, co-manages our photosessions, providing props, costumes, self-designed jewellery, and even her own music. She is a photographer's dream because she has more looks than Lon Chaney. Katrina is a stunning blonde in many of my pictures, but she also appears in a dark-haired incarnation in pieces like AMERICAN ZOMBIE, QUEEN OF LINCOLN BEACH and others.

[1993]

Nereid

Private work. Nereids are
the often malevolent nymphs
of Greek folklore that dwell
in springs or trees,
as well as the sea.
[1992]

Tendrils
of Nightmare

Private work. Strange creatures
from the bottom of the ocean
are always excellent fodder
for nightmares.
[1995]

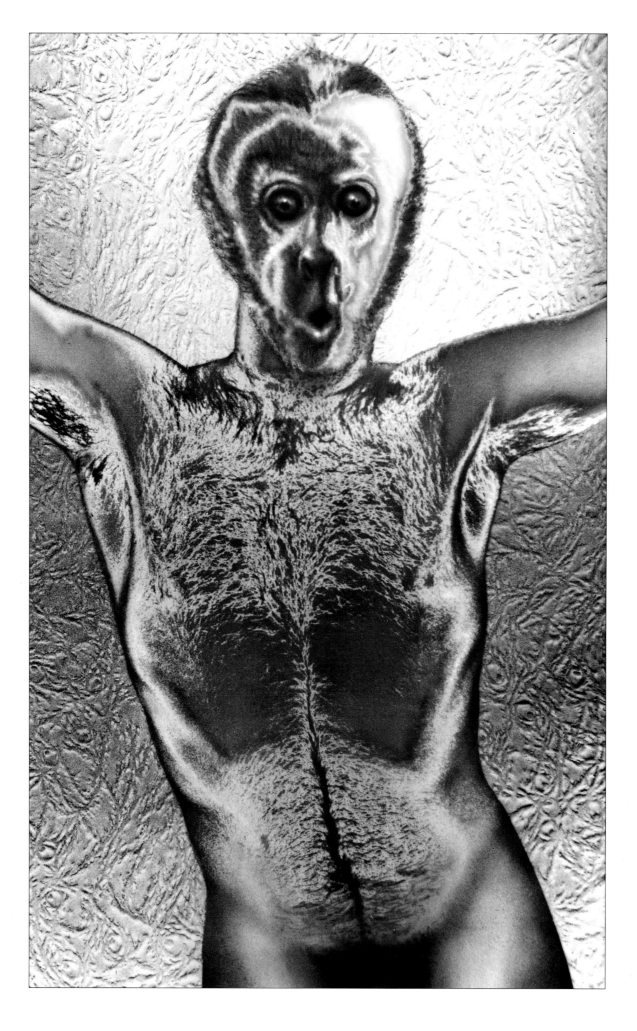

*S*hock Monkey

A naked homunculus with the face of an elderly white-throated Capuchin monkey. Illustration for the novel Who Made Stevie Crye? by Michael Bishop, Arkham House.

[1983]

*R*ed Dreams

This beautiful queen of the underworld speaks through her upraised hand as the white flames flicker through her red dominion. Cover design for Night Cry magazine, later used on a paperback edition of Red Dreams by Dennis Etchison.

[1986]

Filly

Private work. This model is Lisa Carver, whom I first met in a Bourbon Street strip club. Lisa is a lithe and alluring dancer with a small tattoo on the left side of her derrière that reads 'Property of Dracula'. Needless to say, she is a very unusual person. Lisa is the model in NEREID, SPACED, TAPDANCER and many others.

[1995]

Purebred

Private work. One afternoon, a long-time collaborator and friend, Chuck Reily, who had just broken up with his girlfriend, asked me if I needed any pictures of someone overcome by sadness and consumed by despair. The face on the bull came from the photosession which followed.

[1995]

*N*eurotica is the name I have chosen to represent the strange, grotesque and erotic portraits that permeate this book, and most particularly this final chapter. The descent into the abyss began when I first met the highly confrontational performance artist Lydia Lunch, and ended with a series of photosessions with controversial writer and self-described 'non-operable transsexual' Poppy Z. Brite. In between, other notable collaborators stood before my camera, but ironically, some of the people most responsible for the twisted tenor of this volume are nowhere to be found amongst its pages. Actually this is not an entirely accurate statement, since many of their portraits remain, despite the absence of their smiling faces, and this is one of the central mysteries of *Neurotica.*

The late master photographer Clarence John Laughlin often expressed the idea that photography could be used as a tool for self-therapy. The camera can provide a window into the subconscious, revealing a world of personal symbolism that can be used to illumine the darkest corners of the psyche. I have certainly taken this philosophy to heart. Most of the images in this book are products of my own imagination, spun off the top of my head in an attempt to vent my spleen and cleanse my mind. In this effort I have been only partially successful, for I have learned that nightmares can breed more nightmares, and I feel yet worse things waiting in my roiling backbrain.

In addition to my personal work, I have included in this collection of *Neurotica* many book illustrations and covers inspired by the works of Clive Barker, Stephen King, Dennis Etchison, Ramsey Campbell and Douglas E. Winter among others. The tortured imaginations of these writers have made a powerful impression on my own, and I felt these illustrations would complement my personal work quite nicely.

Chapter Four
«NEUROTICA»

Carnal
Chameleon
Private work. If this lizard hadn't yawned fortuitously at the precise moment I took his picture, this image would never have been possible.
[1992]

*T*ransmogrified
Nude Seated on Futon
Private work. This picture took several years to create and it changed shape many times before I settled on this final version.
[1995]

I am bored with endless depictions of women being menaced by monsters, cringing princesses clutching the legs of over-muscled heroes, and submissive glamour girls just waiting to be ravished. Many of the females in my photos would be just as likely to kill you as to kiss you. It's no accident that I have chosen some very strong and intelligent women as the subjects of my photographs. Some might argue that these portraits are still exploitive and that I am making women into monsters, but some of these women *are* monsters and some women *want* to be monsters. I am only too happy to oblige them.

Being a paperback cover artist, I've also done more than my fair share of macho portraits of men wielding guns and other symbolic weaponry. Swords, guns, big muscles, and heroic posing are not really my cup of tea, however, and I would rather leave those themes to others. I prefer my male models to be lean, dark, slightly demented characters, who instinctively go against the grain. The ability to snarl through clenched teeth and scream on cue

are always definite assets, but being able to effect a calculated look of boredom or ennui is equally useful.

Unfortunately the nude male figure is much more a taboo in our society than the female, and this partially accounts for the disproportionate ratio of women to men in this book.

Where would I be without my models? Actually, I don't even like the word model because, rightly or wrongly, it conjures up images of the vacuous and superficial. I consider many of the people I work with to be collaborators. Some of them are already walking works of art in themselves.

I love to indulge the exhibitionistic tendencies of people who like nothing better than to be photographed. I don't have the time to coax shy wallflowers or the painfully self-conscious in front of my lens. I prefer people who are neither afraid nor ashamed of themselves. Sometimes I get more than I bargain for. Occasionally someone will take off their clothes during a photosession whether I want them to or not, but this neither surprises nor disturbs me. I simply want my collaborators to be free to express themselves.

Palmyra
Private work. Inspired by
the idea that ghosts and spirits
often dwell in trees.
[1993]

*M*iss Global Cataclysm
Private work. A modern satire of the pin-up art
of the 40s and 50s, which was popular with the soldiers
who fought in the wars of that era. This admittedly
sick concept was meant to be darkly humorous
and ironic.
[1994]

Siren of Titan

Private work. Portrait of
Lydia Lunch with the head
of a Titan powerlessly
groaning at her feet.

[1995]

Felinity

Private work. Some of the best
photographs I have ever taken have been
of the legendary Lydia Lunch, who was
fanning the flames of inspiration for me
long before she enraptured me in person.
Lydia is a poet, writer, performance
artist and political firebrand,
who is known for the sheer
intensity of her work.

[1993]

Mr. Puckerflex

Private work. Mr. Puckerflex was crowned 'Mr. Alternative Universe' in the interstellar body-building competitions held on the dark side of the moon in 1975.
[1993]

Nimbus

Cover design for the excellent novel of the same title by Alexander Jablokov. The art director.gave me a simple instruction: 'We need a strong image of a man morphing into liquid metal'. Avon Books.
[1993]

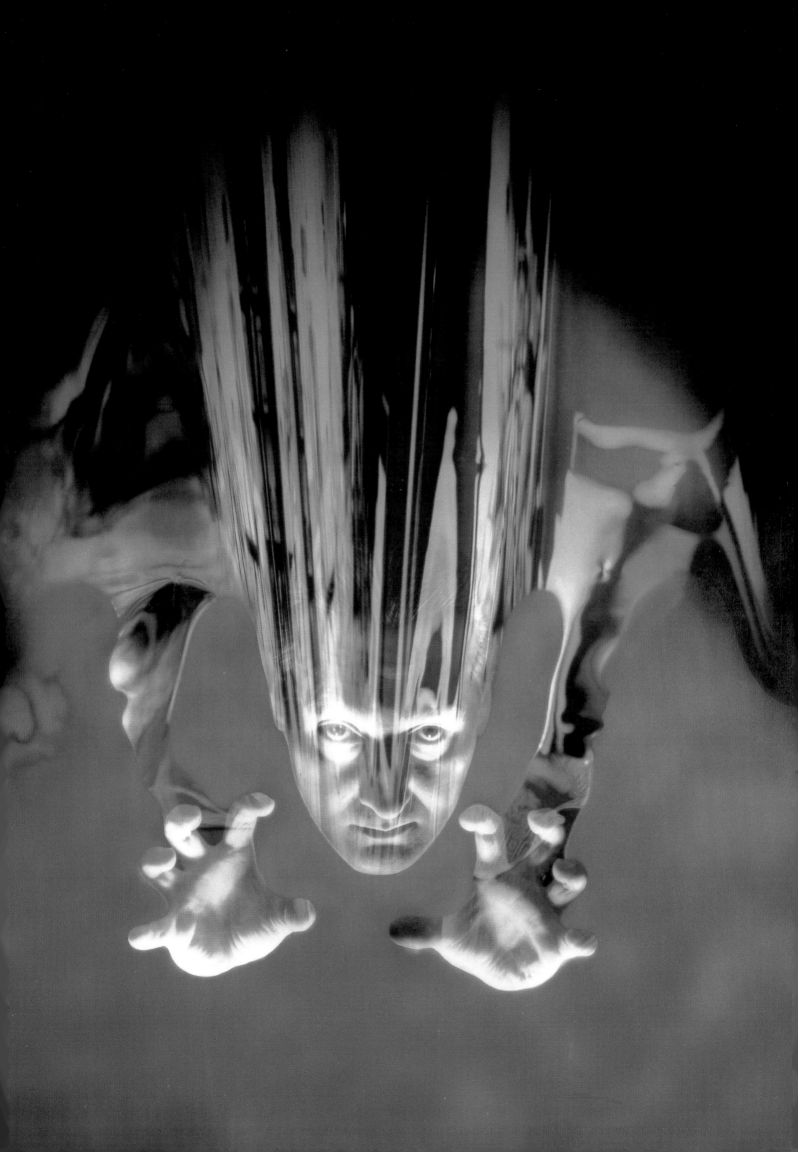

Solarized Portrait

Private work. This is a solarized portrait of Katrina Uribe wearing a surplus gas mask cover as a skirt.

[1993]

Madame Sabattier

Private work. Another solarized picture of Katrina from the same photosession. The circuit board jewellery in the foreground was provided by the model.

[1993]

Alien Miscegenation

Private work. This is a complicated mélange of elements from six different negatives and four different photosessions.

[1991]

Mirror Phantasm

Private work. The great photographer Weegee used to tell people that he created his warped special effects with an elastic lens. I was inspired to create my own distorted photographs after viewing the works of Weegee and Andrew Kertesz.

`[1992]

California Gothic

An illustration for Dennis Etchison's fine novel, California Gothic. The negative image of palm trees in this picture makes a striking design, but I remember them more for the beautiful parrots that were building nests in the treetops the day I took this photo.

[1995]

Jude in Flames

This photo of an exotic dancer performing on the bar of a Bourbon Street nightclub was enhanced with airbrush to create the cover design for California Gothic, Dream Haven Books.

[1995]

Stages

An illustration for
a truly frightening story
by Ramsey Campbell
about hallucinogenic drugs
and voyeurism.
From Scared Stiff,
Scream/Press.
[1987]

The Epiphenomena of Morphogenesis

Illustration for a story written by
David C. Kopaska-Merkel, originally
published in Night Cry magazine
(Fall, 1986). This picture features
the image of a crow which has
popped up in several of my
other illustrations.
[1986]

Soul Effigy

Private work. I've always
loved sculpture, from ancient
examples to Bernini, Brancusi
and Moore. This is a sculpture
design that I lack the talent
to execute in three-dimensional
form. In my mind I envision it
being about 15 metres tall.
[1995]

Idol

Private work.
A modern version
of the ancient
fertility idol.
[1995]

Primal #2

Neanderthal skulls
and a very unpleasant
transformation
make up this piece,
which appeared
as a back cover for
an issue of the
comic book Primal,
Dark Horse
Publishing.
[1993]

The Changelings

Private work. The alterations
in form are proportional to
the amount of alcohol present
in the bloodstreams of
these changelings.
[1995]

Brite in Tatters

Private work. Portrait of Poppy Z. Brite,
the last person I photographed for this book,
and the inspiration for the next eight pages
of images. This picture and the one below
were taken during my final photosession in
a ruined amusement park that was for
many years my favourite shooting location.
It was a bitter-sweet moment when
I left that wonderfully strewn
pile of wreckage for
the last timè.
[1993]

Alone in the Ruins

Private work. I must have
photographed a dozen different
models in the antique dress
that Poppy wears in these scenes.
Without asking her to remove it,
I ripped it on the spot with
a pocket knife, for its final
shredded appearance.
[1993]

Cool Whip on a Cold Corpse

Private work. Poppy looks down at a twentieth century death mask as she contemplates her future, and yours!

[1994]

Poppy, Victoria and Albert

Private work. A photograph from one of the plaster rooms in the Victoria and Albert Museum, London, was used as the background for this portrait.

[1994]

Double
Portrait
Private work.
A simple
double exposure
that required
very little
airbrushing
in the
final print.
[1993]

*P*oppy Z. Brite
Private work. Poppy is a controversial
novelist and short story writer whose dark work
has often managed to shock this jaded,
world-weary horror illustrator.
The diminutive and exquisite Ms Brite can dissect
a reader's brain with her poetically vibrant,
surgically precise prose style.
Personally, I believe she can destroy
your mind with her looks alone.
[1993]

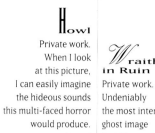

Howl

Private work.
When I look
at this picture,
I can easily imagine
the hideous sounds
this multi-faced horror
would produce.

[1993]

Wraith in Ruin

Private work.
Undeniably
the most intense
ghost image
that I have ever
photographed.

[1993]

108

Skin of Her Teeth

Private work. A recumbent portrait of Poppy used as an illustration for an interview with her that appeared in the magazine Mondo 2000.

[1993]

Height of the Scream

Private work. A picture solely inspired by the title of a Ramsey Campbell book. Often just a title or phrase will be enough to conjure up an image.

[1990]

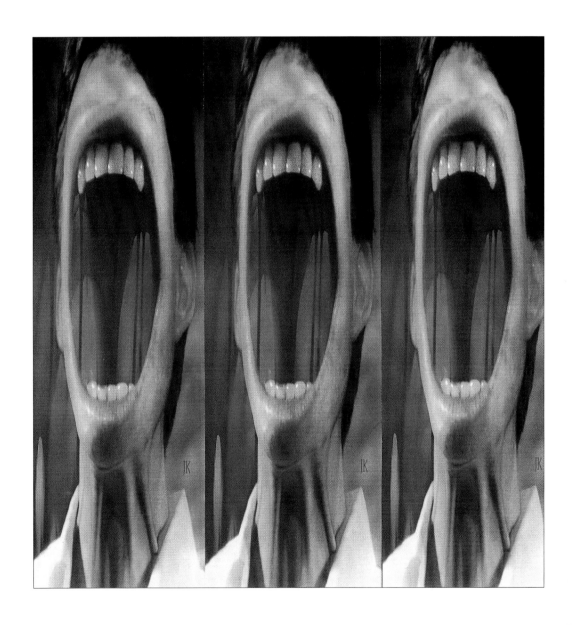

Groucho de Sade
Private work. This title was suggested by
the model, who said he thought he looked
like a cross between Groucho Marx
and the Marquis de Sade
in this picture.
[1990]

Hand of Doom
Private work. Another laborious
reconstruction of a scene from
one of my bad dreams.
[1993]

Mandala

Private work. A biomorphic
mandala designed for a drummer
friend for use as a decorative
bass drum head.

[1992]

Quadruped

Private work. A concept inspired
by Hans Bellmer's surrealistic
doll photographs.

[1991]

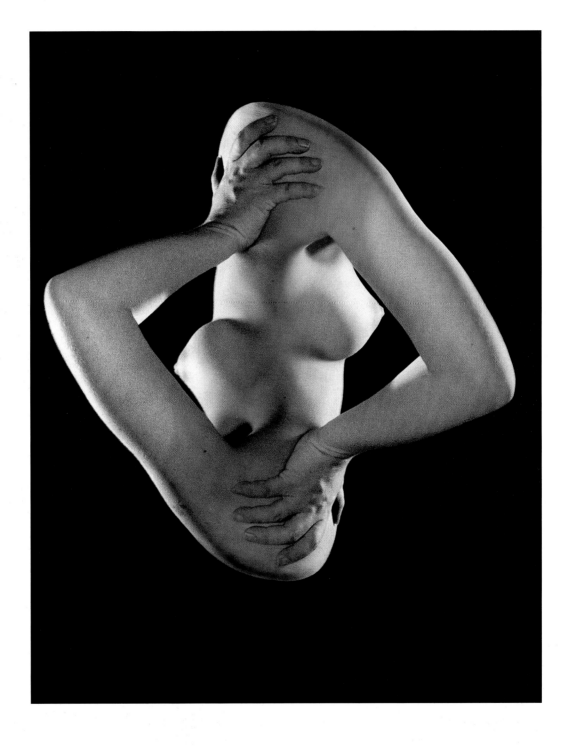

Mutant
**Descending
Staircase**

Private work. The Polish writer
Stanislaw Lem wrote about a future
where people change the shape
and design of their bodies to suit
the fashions of the moment.
Now it seems that this unlikely
scenario is at least partially coming
true in the computerized world of
Cyberspace, where you don't have
to be yourself, you can be your
spirit animal, a toaster with wings,
or some other fanciful version
of yourself.
[1995]

*T*apdancer
Private work. I included
the candlestick in this picture
because it seemed to be
stylistically related to
the figure of the girl
on the hand.
[1992]

Birth of
the Dream
Private work. The background
is a natural double exposure
created by a simple reflection
in window glass.
[1992]

*T*he Egotist
Private work. His unrestrained
arrogance and bloated ego
masked an inner fragility that I knew
would eventually crack open,
like Humpty Dumpty
falling off a wall.
[1995]

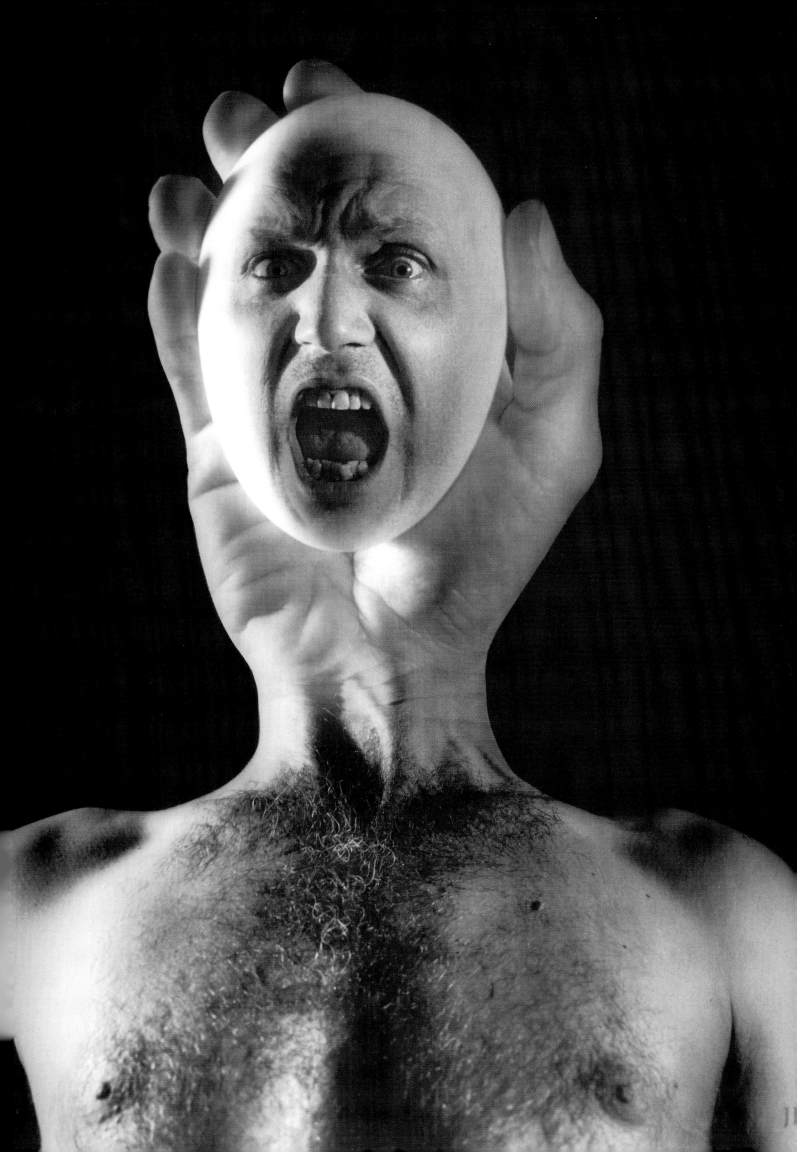

Victim and Clues

Private work. This is a partial photogram,
which is a cameraless image created
by laying objects directly on photographic
paper and exposing them to light.

[1992]

*H*ouse on Fire:
Portrait of J.G.Thirlwell

Private work. Jim Thirlwell, AKA Clint Ruin and
Foetus Interruptus, is a well-known recording artist,
composer and graphic artist who is one of my heroes.
I frequently rely on his music for 'attitude adjustments'
in the darkroom. This piece was inspired by
his song 'Haus on Fah'.

[1995]

ᖴear-Stricken

Private work. This photo and the one below were taken in an isolated ruin of the sort I usually favour. As I was shooting, the model Katrina and I became somewhat distressed as we heard a gang of rowdy youths approaching. Katrina, who was only partially clad, cringed in fear as she hid behind part of a wall, while I photographed her. Luckily the interlopers passed by without seeing us.

[1993]

ᖶhe Cringe

Private work. I originally tried to incorporate fantastic elements into these pictures, but in the end I rejected them in favour of the straight unretouched versions, which are very beautiful by themselves.

[1993]

The Other Side

Illustration for a Ramsey Campbell story created with a strobe light and a long time exposure.

[1986]

Lasher

Private work. He looked normal enough, but when his lips parted, a long slimy tentacle came sliding out of his mouth in place of a tongue.

[1995]

SOME NOTES ON TECHNIQUE

*T*HE QUESTION
I am most often asked about my work is
what kind of computer I use to get my
effects. Although I think the digital revo-
lution is the greatest thing since instant
water, I still favour the old-fashioned
darkroom techniques of multiple printing, multiple exposure, and solarization
for producing my images. I am also very
fond of collage and airbrush techniques,
and enjoy hand-colouring my photos.
All of the full-colour work in this book
started out in black-and-white, and was
then coloured by hand. Some of the
monochromatic pieces were chemically
toned in the darkroom.

Multiple printing is the printing of
different elements from different negatives on one sheet of photographic paper.
I literally reach into the cone of light
projected by my negative enlarger and
blend image components together by
blocking off areas on the paper with
shadows, usually cast by my hands.
Aside from the careful planning and
exposure calculations that go into this

technique, the basic act of multiple
printing involves wiggling fingers and
chopping the air within this projected
beam of light. It's a curious way to go
about fusing different images together —
sort of a Tai Chi shadowplay acted out
in the weak amber light of the darkroom.
This act of merely 'touching' the light in
order to change it in the final image is
to me the most exciting part of printing
photographs.

Solarization, or the Sabattier effect as
it is more properly called, combines both
positive and negative characteristics in
the same image. This surreal, psychedelic
effect creates a partial or total reversal
of tones when the sensitive photographic
paper or film is re-exposed to light during
development. To put it simply, solarization is something of a controlled accident
accomplished by turning the light on in
the darkroom when you really shouldn't.
As you can imagine, this is a very dodgy
technique, which doesn't always work
and you can easily ruin your film or
paper. You can solarize images much
more reliably with the proper software
or video effects generator, but I prefer
the old-fashioned methods which inject
an element of random chance into the
process. To me this is far more romantic,
despite being somewhat inefficient.

Double or multiple exposure, my
favourite technique, is familiar to all of
us. It simply involves taking two or more
pictures on the same sheet of film. The
variety of effects is infinite and the sim-
plicity of execution makes this the most
magical of all the techniques I employ.

Collage, or cut and paste as it is
sometimes called, is like a cross between
making paper dolls and performing sur-
gery on photographs. Images are simply
assembled in pieces and then rephoto-
graphed and retouched.

I like to photograph my own source
material rather than resorting to the
lazy habit of chopping up magazines and
books, and photograph 99 per cent of
the images used in my work, although
I will occasionally borrow a castle or
other image off an old postcard.

Besides the camera, the paintbrush
and airbrush are indispensable tools of
my trade, and I quite enjoy splashing
paint and dye onto my photographs.

There are many tricks and methods
I employ. A few, I'm proud to say are
unique to my work, but most of them
were invented by great photographic
pioneers like Henry Peach Robinson,
William Mortenson, Weegee, Man Ray
and Jerry Uelsmann.

I consider myself a low-tech garage

artist. If I was a musician, I'd be using pawnshop guitars, tube amplifiers and homemade tape loops. My darkroom is very small and unimposing – I use only one enlarger and a small fibreglass sink that leans against the wall when not in use. All of my equipment was bought used and I own very little in the way of fancy electronics. I like to use equipment that I can fix and maintain myself.

I have tried to learn my techniques well enough to forget about them, since the most important thing to me is the emotional and psychological aspect of capturing moods and evoking specific feelings. I am particularly interested in the subtleties of human facial expres-sions and body language, and am also fascinated by the volume of communica-tion conveyed by the eyes alone, which I think is reflected in my work.

Because the camera is so widely used, it is often naively assumed that we know everything there is to know about photo-graphy and the effect of filmed images on the human mind. Photography has only been with us since the early part of the nineteenth century. Compared to the venerable disciplines of drawing and painting, photography is still a very young art form, and one that we have only just begun to understand. Because we are barraged daily with a profusion of video and film images, we tend to take this magic for granted. The camera has changed us – sometimes for the better, sometimes for the worse. Computerized synthesis of imagery, virtual reality, and other technical innovations promise to change us further.

My camera has changed me irrevocably. When I look back through my mountain-ous negative files, my past resurfaces with sometimes frightening clarity. Despite the joys it often gives me, I some-times wonder if I wouldn't be better off without this visual diary. It's no surprise to me that primitive peoples encounter-ing photography for the first time regard it as a soul-stealing process – in some respects it truly is.

Opposite left
Lydia and Ubermenschen
Private work.
Airbrushed photocollage.
[1995]

Opposite right
Madame Sabattier
Private work.
Solarized portrait.
[1993]

Right
Aftermath
Private work.
Photograph of a public square taken from the top floor of the Pompidou Museum, Paris, and printed through a sheet of melted plastic.
[1993]

𝒜 CKNOWLEDGEMENTS

Special thanks to Ken Wilson for designing this volume,
and Suzanne Raymond, Michael Styborski,
and Hector Plasmic
for special assistance.

Thanks also to:

Dale Ashmun
Henry Baker
Alan Bernhoft
G. Sutton Breiding
Poppy Z. Brite
T.M. Caldwell
Lisa Carver
Tracy Cocoman
Hal Dean
Kirby Gee
John Guidry
Bridget Harms
Susan Haynes
Roy Houston
Amy Jaskolka
Joe Jones
Carole King
Lydia Lunch
Dan Meyer
Zack Miller
Harry O. Morris
Cindy Morrow
Chuck Reily
Robert Ricci
Floyd Robinson
Pippa Rubinstein
Joe Stefko
John Strange
Nigel Suckling
Katrina Uribe
Doug Wirth
Brian Yuzna